TRUST
THE
PROCESS

A Five Step Model to Becoming an Everyday Leader

WILLIE JONES, Ph.D.
TEMPESTT ADAMS, Ph.D.

Trust the Process: A Five Step Model to Becoming an Everyday Leader

© 2021 Dr. Willie C. Jones & Dr. Tempestt R. Adams

ISBN PRINT 978-1-09836-688-9 | ISBN eBOOK 978-1-09836-689-6

TABLE OF CONTENTS

PREFACE

Leadership is one of those words that many believe they understand, but often struggle to articulate. Take a moment to think about what leadership means to you:

- What thoughts come to your mind?

- What individuals, if any do you think about?

- How would you define leadership?

If you are anything like us, early on in our careers, we too struggled to articulate what leadership means. But once we were able to, we noticed an alarming trend (and fallacy): leadership was most often confined to official titles and positions.

This book was born out of frustration with this false notion of leadership. As colleagues for over fifteen years—from our classrooms as students at North Carolina State University, to the halls of the schools where we were teachers, to our varied corporate and nonprofit experiences—we know that a title does not always make a good leader, nor does the lack of a title discredit good leaders. So, we channeled our collective experiences to create this work for you. In creating this work, our quintessential goal was to ensure that you gain a better understanding of how to be a more effective leader. This goal was vital to us because we recognize that better leaders result in a better world.

We believe that everyone is a leader. Specifically, we believe that everyone is an everyday leader. Although "everyday leader" is common corporate jargon, we define everyday leadership as *ownership of one's inherent capability to influence self and others.* Everyday leaders first acknowledge themselves as a leader. Next, an everyday leader works to improve their leadership skills before, lastly, working to help others along the way.

This book is different from other leadership texts because we unveil a practical, outcome-based model that you can immediately implement into your work and home life. We were intentional about creating something that we felt was a quick read since, in today's fast-paced, ever-changing, global world, learning agility is imperative for individuals and organizations to operate efficiently. Thus, this "take it and run with it" approach was important to us so that our model will be mentally empowering and delivered in a manner that allows you to immediately put what you learn into action.

This book is organized into five chapters. Each chapter reviews a component of the five-step model we have created to help you *trust the process*. We intentionally decided to use a storytelling approach throughout the book to make elements of the model more relatable. Furthermore, we found this approach to be most applicable, considering this model was created from our lived experiences as we continuously work to become everyday leaders. In the book, you will learn from the leadership stories of Dave, Andrew, Amanda, and Tessa (pseudonyms of course). It should be noted that because of our unique individual experiences, there are occasional changes of voice from "I" to "we" throughout the book. We believe you will find our model beneficial as you work to be a better leader today, tomorrow, and every day thereafter.

INTRODUCTION

"If your actions inspire others to dream more, learn more, do more and become more, you are a leader."
~President John Quincy Adams

Picture this:

It's your first day on a brand new job—your dream job—the one you've always wanted. You've heard great things about the company culture, and employees who work there often go on to do amazing work. With a big smile, you enter the building for the first time. You are promptly greeted by the administrative assistant, John. John is seemingly startled by your arrival and shares that he was not expecting you for another week. Nevertheless, he escorts you to your new workspace (which is unfinished) and shares that Dave, your new boss, has not yet arrived but should be arriving any moment now. A couple of hours pass and there are still no signs of Dave. At this time, you begin to wonder, "Why wasn't John prepared for my arrival? Did I misread the paperwork? Am I actually a week early?" As your mind continues to race, you hear voices in the distance, one of which says, "Good Morning, Dave. Your new employee started today and is patiently awaiting your arrival."

Moments later, Dave approaches you and apologizes for his tardiness. He proceeds into his office and closes the door for the next hour or so. After some time has passed, Dave opens his door and says to you, "How are things going?" Still excited, you exchange pleasantries, engage in small talk, and ask, "What would you like for me to work on, Dave?" Unprepared for the question, Dave stammers for a bit and then manages to find a 10-page marketing booklet that is typically provided to customers. Dave says, "Here read this. This

1

entails what we do as a company. It should probably take you the rest of today to finish." At this point, it's almost lunchtime. Upon returning from lunch, you cynically begin planning how to read a whole 10-page marketing booklet in just 4 hours. The day concludes, and you look forward to a new start tomorrow morning.

It's the following day and you arrive promptly at 8am. There are no signs of Dave. Having read and reread the 10-page marketing materials provided to you the day before, you begin getting anxious for your next assignment. Dave arrives around 9am and heads straight into his office. After some time passes, eager to show your value, you work up the courage to enter Dave's office and ask him for your next assignment. Again, caught off guard, Dave stammers and says, "Well, have you finished reading the booklet?" While smiling, you assure Dave that you have read (and reread) the booklet thoroughly. Dave replies, "Great! Well, now that you've completed orientation, you should know exactly what we do as a company and what needs to be done moving forward. Let me know if you have any questions about next steps, but if you've read the booklet, there probably shouldn't be any questions." A bit confused and perplexed, you walk back to your workspace.

Leadership Defined – The Everyday Leader

Sadly enough, this story is based on true events. In fact, I lived it. While reading the story, what were your thoughts about my interactions with Dave? What was your perception of Dave? Did you perceive him to be a leader? If you're like me, your perception of Dave was not very favorable. Over the next several months, working for Dave turned what should have been a dream job into a nightmare. This ultimately resulted in me jumping ship to join another company. But, my answer to the question, "Did you perceive him to be a leader?", might surprise you. The answer is *yes* and I will explain why.

Leadership is not about power, authority, or titles. Simply put, leadership is about influence. In fact, John Maxwell, who has authored many books including *The 21 Irrefutable Laws of Leadership,* proclaims "Leadership is influence – nothing more, nothing less." So, in reflecting on the question and answering it objectively: Yes, Dave is a leader. Dave's influence was powerful enough to result in me leaving my "dream job" to join another company. Take a moment to let that sink in; Dave's leadership was so impactful that he was able to influence me to leave my job. The point here is that when leadership is expressed as one's ability to influence, the title of "leader" becomes available to anyone and everyone, including you. In Dave's case, negative influence was exerted; yet, Dave is a leader.

One blaring drawback in Maxwell's explanation of leadership is that it does not delineate good leadership from bad leadership, and here is where we will bridge the gap. In writing this book, we intend to provide you with a more practical definition of what leadership is, share real stories of both good and bad leadership in action, and unveil a simple five-step model to becoming an everyday leader. In Dave's story, his leadership was not exemplary; it resulted in losing what could have been a valuable employee. By sharing more stories like Dave's and the valuable leadership lessons learned from real-life experiences, our quintessential goal is to ensure that you gain a better understanding of how to be a more effective leader. To accomplish this goal, we will break down our five-step model to becoming an everyday leader into digestible chunks that can be integrated into how you, your peers, your team, and/or individuals within your organization behave every day. Whether you are a leader in Corporate America, a leader in the classroom, a community leader, an emerging leader, or simply a leader of self, this book is for you. We promise that if you read this book with an open mind, critically reflect on the content, and implement the strategies shared, you WILL become a more engaging and impactful leader.

Now, to help paint a clearer picture of how we will define leadership for the remainder of this book, let's start by reviewing a few perspectives from reputable practitioners.

Simon Sinek, the author of many bestsellers including Start with Why, expressed that "Leadership is about making others feel safe...Leadership is a choice, not a rank." Warren Bennis, a distinguished Professor and Founding Chairman of The Leadership Institute at the University of Southern California shared that, "Leadership is the capacity to translate vision into reality." Peter Northouse, Professor Emeritus of Communication at Western Michigan University and author of countless leadership books, defined leadership as "a process whereby an individual influences a group of individuals to achieve a common goal."

In building on the preceding definitions, we define leadership as *an outcome-based process in which an individual intentionally opts to exert direct or indirect influence over another individual or group of individuals.* When leadership is defined in this manner, as an outcome-based process in which one intentionally opts to exert influence, it becomes available to anyone and everyone willing to learn and execute the process. This includes you, the everyday leader. As such, we define everyday leadership as *ownership of one's inherent capability to influence self and others.* To distinguish good leadership from bad leadership, we propose that good leadership produces a positive outcome and is the result of positive intentions. Whereas, bad leadership may produce a positive or negative outcome and be the result of positive or negative intentions. Allow us to explain.

In the results-driven world that we live in, if you cannot produce positive outcomes, you cannot call yourself a good leader. With a heightened sense of attention being placed on ethical leadership, if you do not display positive intent, you cannot call yourself a good leader. Conversely, a leader can display negative intent, but still manage to produce positive outcomes. However, due to the lack of ethics displayed by said leader, we deem this to be bad leadership. In short, bad leadership can produce good or bad outcomes and be the result of good or bad intent; yet, good leadership is an intentional process that must produce positive outcomes and be the result of positive intent.

The Process

The ideology of becoming an everyday leader is simple, yet many organizations are filled with individuals who fail to think and act like a leader. This failure results in organizations spending an inordinate amount of time and money on the development needs of individuals. In fact, according to the Association for Talent Development (ATD), their 2017 *State of the Industry* report "found that organizations spent $1,273 per employee in 2016." This is a dollar amount that has steadily increased year-over-year since 2011. The *State of the Industry Report* suggests that smaller organizations pay a higher average cost per employee. Specifically, the data showed:

- Small organizations (fewer than 500 employees), spent an average of $2,016 per employee on learning

- Midsize organizations (between 500 to 9,999 employees) spent $973

- Large organizations (a minimum of 10,000 employees) spent $673.

Despite the smaller percentages spent on learning, larger organizations "saw their employees use more learning hours, on average, than workers at midsize and small organizations" and "the average cost per learning hour available across all organizations was $1,809."

While understanding that Human Capital (and the upskilling of this capital) is critical to the long-term sustainability of any viable organization, we propose a more cost-efficient, practical solution.

Our solution consists of a five-step model that can be learned, taught, implemented, and adopted to ensure that you, your peers, your team, individuals within your organization, and even your loved ones think and act like a leader, every day.

The Five-Step Model for Everyday Leadership

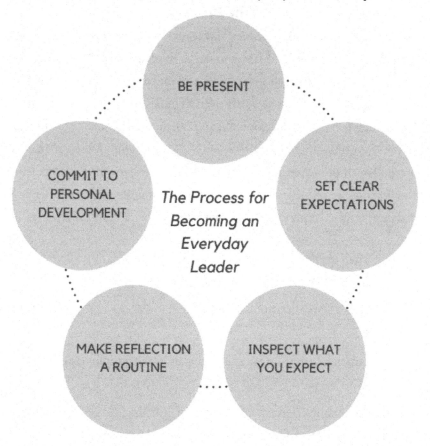

Our five-step model was designed to provide an iterative approach to becoming an everyday leader. The model can be applied in a nonlinear manner which allows you to diagnose your specific needs and prescribe the appropriate remedy. Yet, for this book, the model will be unveiled sequentially for ease of understanding. Throughout this book, we will equip you with the right tools, resources, and knowledge to decipher where you are in the process and accordingly, what behaviors you must adopt. Remembering that leadership is an outcome-based process in which an individual must intentionally opt to exert influence over another individual or group of individuals, our model reveals five intentional and learnable steps: (1) Be Present, (2) Set Clear Expectations, (3) Inspect What You Expect, (4) Reflect on the Process, and (5) Commit to Personal Development. In essence, to become an everyday leader and personify the quote shared at the onset of this chapter, you must be intentional and take action that inspires others to dream more, learn more, and become more. In the chapters that follow, our five-step model to becoming an everyday leader will be unveiled through storytelling and reflections on lessons learned from past experiences. Throughout each chapter, we will provide tips and strategies to assist you with efforts to implement the model. Accordingly, we propose your first action be to *Trust the Process* and focus your efforts on mastering the five steps for becoming an everyday leader.

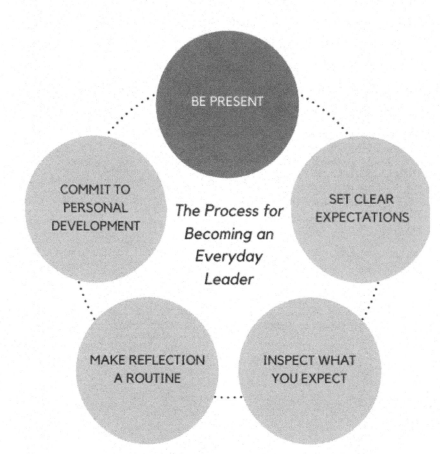

CHAPTER 1: BE PRESENT

"Awareness is like the sun. When it shines on things, they are
transformed."
~Thich Nhat Hanh

Like most professionals, as a college professor, I am often tasked with competing priorities. From planning and leading class discussions, reviewing countless emails, conducting research, grading assignments, having one-on-one meetings with my students, or simply meeting with my department head, there is rarely enough time in the day to complete everything on my to-do list.

Accordingly, one day after class, I stopped by my department head's office to discuss a minor concern. In failing to formally schedule time on her calendar, it was blatantly obvious to me that my arrival had inadvertently interrupted her workflow. I apologized profusely. But, at that moment, her response left a lasting imprint on me and served as an example of the leader I strive to become. What struck me most about her response was the genuinely pleasant, calm, and welcoming demeanor I was met with. Though in the middle of what was probably some vastly important work, she welcomed me into her office, told me to have a seat at the conference table, and proceeded to be completely *present*. The conversation did not last more than 10 minutes, but how she made me feel in that exact moment will last a lifetime. Throughout the conversation, she allowed me to express my concern without interruption, remained attentive, and actively listened. It was an extremely helpful conversation that focused solely on me and my needs. After taking a moment to reflect on the conversation, I recalled a few things about her:

- She came to the table empty-handed. She previously had a book in her hand, but she put it down.

- Her cell phone was on her desk, but it never made it to the conference table.

- Her eye contact was impeccable.

- Her cell phone buzzed a few times. Thinking it might be of importance, I asked if she needed to get it; but she assured me it could wait.

- She was visibly attentive throughout the conversation.

After this quick reflection, I was immediately reminded of a time, about a week before this conversation, when I was in a scheduled meeting with a student. The student arrived at my office prepared to discuss some minor project details for the course. I was able to offer clarity, review her progress, and provide some pertinent feedback. But, after the meeting concluded, I felt guilty because even though this was a scheduled meeting:

- My email was still open on my desktop and I glanced at it a couple of times.

- My text alerts were going off and I felt the need to respond because my husband and I were in the middle of a home renovation project that I could not stop thinking about.

- I asked her to repeat herself once or twice because mid-sentence I realized I was not fully present.

In comparing the two interactions, there is one obvious difference: my department head was more present for me in an impromptu meeting than I was for my student in a scheduled meeting. Acknowledging this brutal reality was not easy, but the increased awareness of my own shortcoming served as a catalyst for changing my behavior. Being present is a learnable skill that improves once you acknowledge your shortcomings, and commit to identifying triggers that prevent you from reaching an optimal level of self-awareness.

From these examples alone, we are confident you can begin to understand the need to be present. Still, with this newfound understanding, it is imperative that we clearly articulate what it means to be present. To be present means to focus 100% of your attention on the person speaking so they can be fully heard and understood without any distractions. Being present means intentionally listening, suspending judgment, and observing all elements of communication, both verbal and nonverbal. Accomplishing this first step in the process of becoming an everyday leader is difficult because it requires you to refrain from natural tendencies to fix problems, avoid offering unwarranted advice, resist formulating answers in your head, and abstain from daydreaming about what you're going to say next or do later on that day. Don't believe me? Think back to the last time a friend, significant other, child, colleague, or direct report came to you with a problem or concern.

- Did your mind immediately jump into "fix it" mode?
- Did you ask probing questions that could potentially make them defensive?
- Did you offer unsolicited advice?
- Were you mentally trying to rescue them from the situation?
- While they were talking, did your mind drift or wander at all?
- Did you begin formulating your next question or statement while they were speaking?

If you answered "yes" to any or all of these questions, then you were not being present. Recognizing that being present is a challenge for nearly everyone, we have developed the "AA framework", designed to outline specific behaviors that can help you remember to be present in your everyday interactions. The framework entails **Allowing** yourself to be in the moment and **Actively listening**.

Allow

Allowing yourself the time and space to truly be in the moment is a critical aspect of being present. To accomplish this, we recommend three tips. The first is to identify triggers that detract you from your ability to be fully present. These triggers might include the ringing of an office phone, a text message, an email, an alert on your smartwatch or other smart devices, sidebar conversations, a knock at the door, or even the infamous, "Hey do you have a sec/minute?" Taking a moment to establish an awareness of your trigger(s) will activate the process which allows you to redirect your energy and attention back to what is most important. In speaking of awareness, understanding how other people experience and receive you is another critical aspect of being present. To truly understand how other people experience you, our second tip involves conducting a quick and honest self-assessment by asking yourself the following questions:

- Am I approachable?

- Do I have an open-door policy?

- Am I always direct and honest, even if it isn't what the other person wants to hear?

- Am I transparent, genuine, open, and authentic in my daily interactions?

- Do I apologize when I have made a mistake?

- Do others see me as loyal?

- Do I thank my supervisor, direct reports, colleagues, friends, and/ or family members for their feedback, even if I do not agree with it?

- Do I actively practice accountability and own up when I am in the wrong?

- Have I done the work it takes to build relationships and establish trust?

Completing this quick self-assessment in an honest and forthright manner will assist you in understanding how other people receive you, and allow you to continue the journey of becoming more present in your actions as an everyday leader. The results of this assessment should serve as a starting point by providing you with one or two areas that you can actively work to produce better results. For instance, if you self-identified that your areas of opportunity are being direct and apologizing when you've made a mistake, develop a plan to begin working on these areas to assist you in establishing better relationships.

As trained educators, we learned early in our scholarly programs that in order to lead and teach effectively, establishing relationships is paramount. Hence, establishing relationships is the third tip and it applies not only in the classroom, but in other aspects of your work and life as well. To establish better relationships, try conducting periodic individual check-ins with those you interact with frequently, showing a genuine interest in the interests of others, fostering goodwill, and being authentic. Of all the immensely important ideas provided for establishing better relationships, the one we most highly recommend is authenticity. Family, friends, students, employees, peers, colleagues, direct reports, and supervisors can all tell when someone is being fake. If identified as "fake", you risk quickly losing credibility and any remaining social capital that you have. When reflecting and preparing your approach to being present, *allow* yourself the time and space needed to truly be in the moment. To accomplish this, remember the aforementioned tips: (1) identify your triggers, (2) conduct an honest self-assessment, and (3) establish authentic relationships.

Utilize Active Listening Strategies

In your journey to becoming an everyday leader, it is imperative that you provide uninterrupted attention in those moments when it is most needed. Be like the department chair, not the professor! This seems simple in theory, but we know that in reality you are being pulled in so many directions at the same time and are often battling sensory and information overload. To combat this overload, utilizing active listening strategies can help ensure you are remaining attentive throughout your conversation. First, at the start of a conversation try addressing your triggers head-on, as referenced above. Again, without awareness of those triggers, your ability to be attentive and listen actively will be impacted.

That said, most of us think we are great listeners. But if you are any-thing like me, you may have realized after reading this chapter that you are not as good as you thought. Taking this a step further, I realized I am often a good listener in certain situations; a selective listener if you will. To combat this, utilizing active listening strategies can ensure the people we serve not only feel like they are being heard, but also feel like they are being listened to. We know that listening takes actual concentration to process. There is a lot of information available about active listening but for ease and immediate implementation, we suggest the following tips:

1. **Zoom in.** Make sure that you focus on the person and listen intently to their conversation. When you zoom in, you are mind-ful of your triggers and you block out distractions to give the speakers your undivided attention.

2. **Engage appropriately.** This requires some form of response, starting with verbal and nonverbal cues. Consider the signals you are sending to the speaker based on body language and the use of audible responses such as "I see," "okay," "yes," or "um hum." Also, think about the cues that both negative and positive body language can send.

3. **Ensure your understanding.** Engage in the conversation with the speaker by making sure you are actually receiving and interpret-ing the information accurately. Responses like, "What I think I hear you saying is…" or "Let me take a moment to make sure I understand what you are saying…" are effortless statements that go a long way in helping the person ensure everyone's under-standing. In turn, they signal to the sender that the receiver is listening, while also minimizing any misunderstandings.

4. **Proceed as needed.** By being present, engaging, and ensuring understanding first, you are more likely to be equipped with the empathy, guidance, and/or solutions the speaker needs.

To assist you with becoming a more active listener, we encourage you to take mental notes during your next conversation. After the conversation has ended, use this brief post-assessment to rate yourself on how well you performed:

- Did I formulate answers in my head while the individual was still talking?

- Did I focus on what I was going to say next instead of seeking understanding?

- Did I account for and keep my triggers in check?

If the answer is no to the first two questions, and yes to the last, you are likely demonstrating active listening. Mastering these tips and creating a habit of reflection will greatly improve your capacity to be a fully present, active listener.

When we think about the need to be present as a precursor for success in leadership, we are reminded of one of the first lessons we both learned during our undergraduate orientation at North Carolina State University. We were made aware that the likelihood of our success could be greatly increased if we chose a seat in the "Learning T" of our academic classrooms. What is the Learning T you might ask? The Learning T was made up of the first few horizontal rows in front of the classroom and the 3-5 vertical rows that ran parallel with the professor. Essentially, being present was more likely if we intentionally sat in seats that were more likely to gain the attention of the professor, and indirectly force us to pay attention. This strategy turned out to be true, even in classes with hundreds of students. Using the spirit of this analogy, we encourage you to find and define your own "Learning T" at home and work so that you can be fully present at all times. As the quote at the onset of this chapter states, heightening your awareness and being 100% present will put you on the right path to becoming an everyday leader.

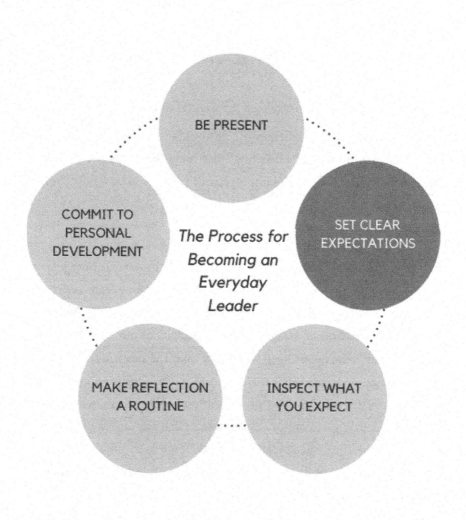

BE PRESENT

COMMIT TO
PERSONAL
DEVELOPMENT

*The Process for
Becoming an
Everyday
Leader*

SET CLEAR
EXPECTATIONS

MAKE REFLECTION
A ROUTINE

INSPECT WHAT
YOU EXPECT

CHAPTER 2: SET CLEAR EXPECTATIONS

"A poor sailor blames the wind."
~John Miller, Author of QBQ

Earlier in my career, I accepted a leadership role within a large organization. Unbeknownst to me, in accepting this position, I was about to inherit a "bad employee" whom we will call Andrew. To make matters worse, this "bad employee" was the manager of about 15 employees so any mistakes or errors in Andrew's judgment were amplified. Fast-forward and it is now day one in my brand-new role as leader. Knowing that it is important to *trust the process*, I spend the first two weeks simply being present. During this time, I allow myself to observe, actively listen, ask questions when appropriate, engage, and ultimately give full attention to all my direct reports, including Andrew. I can vividly remember a one-on-one meeting in which Andrew said, "I've never had a leader actually listen to what I have to say. It is evident that you care about how I feel and my overall development. I could get used to this. This is great."

Now, it would be easy to say, "Andrew was simply kissing up to you and trying to keep his job." But the fact is, in the time I spent simply being present, I came to learn that Andrew had no idea he was viewed as a weak leader by his direct reports, peers, and previous leadership. You might be wondering, how can I be so sure that Andrew was oblivious to his reputation? Well, the evidence emerged during our one-on-one meeting when Andrew shared frustrations of being overlooked for promotion after promotion. Andrew was completely baffled as to what he was doing wrong and asked for my input. It was at this moment, after spending 2 long weeks of simply *Being Present,* that I knew it was time to proceed to step 2: Set Clear Expectations.

Set Clear Expectations

In the story of Andrew, I inherited a "bad employee." But, from my perspective, there is no such thing as a bad employee. Instead, I would argue that there is simply a misalignment between the employee's skills and the actual needs of the role. In these instances, I subscribe to the common workplace mantra of *coach them up or coach them out*. Accordingly, when coaching, expectations must be set and clearly understood by all involved parties. Throughout the remainder of this chapter, Andrew's story will be continued. And, in doing so, we will unveil how you can easily set clear expectations by implementing what we refer to as C5LC or the Critical Five Leadership Competencies: Candor, Calibration, Clarification, Collaboration, and Consolidation.

Candor

Candor can be defined in many ways. Here, we will define it using Kim Scott's concept of *Radical Candor*. In Scott's book, *Radical Candor: Be a Kick-Ass Boss Without Losing Your Humanity*, she expresses that radical candor simply means "challenging directly while also showing that you care personally." In the story of Andrew, it was now time for me to set clear expectations. To accomplish this, I knew that being candid was the only solution. If you will recall, I spent the first two weeks being present and simply building a relationship with Andrew. Essentially, I was showing him that I cared. Consequently, Andrew shared that it was evident I cared about how he felt and his overall development. These sentiments made the following conversation much easier.

During our one-on-one meeting, I said to Andrew, "This might be a bit of a difficult conversation, but I assure you, I have your best interest in mind and will commit to partnering with you to ensure your success. However, I can only commit to this if you're also willing to partner with me." After making this statement, I paused and decided to simply *Be Present*. After a brief moment of silence, Andrew's usual smile turned into a look of concern and he asked, "I'm not getting fired, am I?" With a subtle chuckle and a brief grin, I replied, "No. You are not being fired. But, to be candid, if we don't take the necessary steps to improve your performance, additional action, up to termination, may be taken. Understanding that I have your best interest in mind and don't want to see you fired, would you be willing to partner with me to ensure that this does not happen?" Without hesitation, Andrew responded, "Sure! Just tell me what I need to do, and I'll get it done."

I'll pause the story of Andrew here to reflect briefly on the power of candor. To be candid and challenge someone directly takes courage. However, being courageous is not easy. The alternative, failing to display courage and candor, is a much easier behavior that many leaders choose to display. Let's face it, in uncomfortable situations, it is easier to choose silence. Yet, the decision to choose silence and withhold candor will cause much greater difficulties further down the line than the decision to simply exercise candor. So, we challenge you to become comfortable with your discomfort. And, what better way to ignite this process than by choosing to display courage?

Fortunately, choosing courage and exercising candor are behaviors each of us can learn. In becoming an everyday leader, you must be courageous and fully committed to the practice of candor. Mastering the **art** of candor requires repetition and a willingness to fail fast and often. Of equal importance, mastering the **practice** of candor will quickly increase your leadership influence, credibility, and overall results. As the old saying goes, "People don't care how much you know until they know how much you care." Moving forward, let's take a look at the next critical leadership competency, *calibration*, and see how it was used in Andrew's story.

Calibration

In Julie Zhuo's book, *The Making of a Manager*, she shares that calibration is about "making sure the view we have of ourselves matches reality." Additionally, Zhuo continues by expressing, "Calibration matters because it doesn't do us any good to think that we are one thing when the world views us as another." Zhuo's quotes encapsulate the importance of calibration and why it is a critical leadership competency.

Going back to the story with Andrew, our one-on-one conversation picked up right where we left off, with Andrew giving me his commitment to partner in his success. Unfortunately, it was again time for me to provide Andrew some difficult feedback. This time, the feedback was about how he was viewed by leaders, peers, and direct reports. In short, Andrew was viewed as an extremely nice guy who everyone liked to be around. But, when it came to how he was viewed as a leader and peer, Andrew was viewed as ineffective. Words used to describe him were "doormat", "pushover", "scatterbrained", "conflict-averse", and "inattentive to results."

After delivering the feedback to Andrew, I asked him to recap for me everything he had just heard, but to do so using his own words. At this time, a frustrated Andrew responded with, "So, basically, I am a horrible boss, colleague, and direct report. Got it! And, more than likely, unless I take drastic actions to change, their opinions will lead to me being fired. I think that about sums it up. Did I miss anything?"

Andrew's comments let me know that there was a disconnect between what I shared and what he heard. An important lesson about calibration is, it does not matter if you are calibrating with a direct report, supervisor, peer, or loved one, in becoming an everyday leader, it is critical YOU take ownership for ensuring that the message shared is received as intended and fully understood. To accomplish this, we move to the third critical leadership competency, *clarification*, and discover how it assisted Andrew in gaining a better understanding of how others viewed him.

Clarification

Clarification is a critical leadership competency because when practicing candor, emotions can become highly volatile, often resulting in the receiver of the message displaying a heightened level of sensitivity and/or defensiveness. In the story of Andrew, this heightened level of sensitivity and defensiveness was evident by his tone and word choices such as, "I am a horrible boss," and "…their opinions will lead to me being fired." If/when this occurs, calibration allows both the sender and receiver of the message an opportunity to pause and ensure that there is alignment between intent, perception, and reality. In the likely event that there is any sort of misalignment, clarification is vital.

To be clear, we define clarification as the process by which one proactively clears up any misunderstandings and ensures alignment between intent, perception, and reality of the message being communicated. In this step, being proactive is paramount because in becoming an everyday leader, you must adopt the mindset that any misalignments or misunderstandings are the result of an error in your communication. Adopting this proactive mindset shifts blame from the receiver of the message to you, the sender. By assuming ownership of the miscommunication, the probability of any unnecessary heightened levels of sensitivity and defensiveness are greatly decreased. Additionally, after taking ownership of the miscommunication, you must redirect attention to clarifying intent. At this time, it is extremely tempting to soften your message; but, be cautious of softening your message because soft messages do not teach hard lessons. And at times, a firm stance must be taken to improve negative behaviors and achieve optimal results. When these situations emerge and a stance is required, be sure to focus on being fully present, transparent, and candid.

From Andrew's story, you will remember that Andrew was frustrated. He shared that his perception of my message was, "So, basically, I am a horrible boss, colleague, and direct report…And, more than likely, unless I take drastic actions to change, their opinions will lead to me being fired." Clearly, Andrew's perception of my message was not in alignment with my intent or reality. Consequently, I knew it was imperative for me to clarify my message. In speaking with Andrew, I said,

> No. I am not saying you are a horrible boss, colleague, or direct report. And, I apologize for any miscommunication. The fact is, your direct reports, colleagues, and previous leaders all shared the same

sentiments that you're well-liked, very personable, and a joy to be around. Now, (avoiding the softening trap) what they also shared is you don't make the tough decisions and at times your quest to be well-liked results in you becoming a doormat who lets everyone walk all over you. Would you agree with their assessment, the good and the bad?

Andrew nodded and agreed. I went on to tell Andrew, "Having direct reports, colleagues, and leaders who actually like you is half the battle. But the other half is equally important, and I believe *this* is where you are missing the mark." Andrew asked, "Well, what is the other half and how can I get better?" Before answering this question, I asked Andrew one final clarifying question which was, "Just to make sure we are on the same page, you understand that I am not saying you are a horrible boss, colleague, or direct report, correct?" He nodded in agreement. I said, "Great! Now, let's **collaborate** on the changes **we** need to make to ensure that you are operating at an optimal level."

Collaboration

Collaboration, the fourth critical leadership competency, is a powerful approach to setting clear expectations, but it is often misunderstood. In a recent Harvard Business Review article, *How to Capture Value from Collaboration, Especially If You're Skeptical About It,* Heidi Gardner and Herminia Ibarra expressed that collaboration is "a way of working that attracts and involves people outside one's formal control, organization, and expertise to accomplish common goals." For this book, we will amend this definition to say that collaboration is a way of working that attracts and involves people **inside or** outside one's formal control, organization, and expertise to accomplish **shared expectations**. From our perspective, the same approach that is used outside of one's formal control can be implemented with individuals who are inside one's formal control, organization, and expertise.

22

Now that you have a clearer understanding of how we define collaboration, let's discuss the role it plays in helping you become an everyday leader who sets clear expectations. For starters, when we collaborate, we actively involve others in the process of setting and achieving shared expectations. Later in the book, you will be exposed to an innovative approach to goal-setting called S.M.A.R.T.E.R goals; thus, our focus in this chapter is not to detail the goal setting process. Instead, we merely seek to inform you of the enormous impact that collaboration has on the process of setting clear expectations. To accomplish this, let's further analyze the story of Andrew. When we left off, Andrew was nodding his head in agreement that he fully understood my clarified message. Additionally, he was eagerly awaiting direction as to how he was missing the mark and what could be done to improve his performance.

It is in this moment of truth that many leaders, even some of the most seasoned leaders, make a costly mistake. What mistake, you might ask? The mistake many leaders fall victim to is, like a hero, they swoop in to save the day by providing immediate answers. Conversely, in becoming an everyday leader you must use collaboration as a means to facilitate self-reliant problem solving. The process of self-reliant problem solving shows the individual that they can rely on themselves to solve most problems instead of feeling the need to constantly seek out help.

When working with Andrew, I avoided the costly mistake of being a hero and began the process of collaboration by **asking questions**, not answering questions. Specifically, my approach was to focus on asking "what" and "how" questions because "what" questions generate a more thorough understanding, and "how" questions drive action. To illustrate the point, I asked Andrew, "What do you think makes people say that you don't make tough decisions?" After listening to Andrew's answer, I followed up with, "What can WE do to change that?" The insertion of "we" in the question was intentional and served to further emphasize that this is a collaborative process. As Andrew continued to answer questions, I asked, "How might things look differently if you take an alternative approach?"

Throughout the process, I was present and partnered with Andrew as he answered questions and developed a plan of action. In short, I was facilitating self-reliant problem solving by acting as more of a coach than a hero.

Now, in becoming an everyday leader, it is important to add value and provide direction when the situation warrants it. But, it is equally important that the process is collaborative and not authoritative. As the conversation between Andrew and me continued, I asked, "What would you like for people to say about you as a leader, direct report, peer, loved one, etc.?" Based on Andrew's response, I followed up with the question of, "How can WE make your vision a reality?" In allowing Andrew an opportunity to come up with a plan and together we modify the plan, we were able to set clear expectations. Additionally, Andrew gave 100% buy-in and commitment to the process because he was actively involved in the collaboration.

In full transparency, practicing the art of collaboration is not easy and can at times seem like a slow process. Nonetheless, it is important to remember the intent is to facilitate self-reliant problem solving and ensure 100% buy-in on the task(s) at hand. If you are collaborating with an individual who is not highly competent or committed to the task at hand, you can probe for additional details as to why or why not by using two simple phrases: "Tell me more." and, "How does that make you feel?" Understanding the process can sometimes seem difficult and slow. It is important to remember that in today's workforce, collaboration is not optional, it is a necessity. A recent Harvard Business Review pulse survey, *Meeting the Challenges of Developing Collaborative Teams for Future Success,* reports, "89% of respondents say that prioritizing collaboration and teamwork is increasingly part of their organization's overall workforce strategy." Consequently, in becoming an everyday leader, collaboration is essential, and to accomplish this, it is imperative that you listen, suspend judgment, ask questions, and allow those you are working with an opportunity to actively engage in the process. To follow, Andrew's story concludes with the fifth and final critical leadership competency: ***consolidation***, which further emphasizes the integral process of setting clear expectations.

Consolidation

Consolidation involves bringing together various components or parts into a unified whole. With Andrew, consolidation was accomplished by transferring the abstract to a short list of concrete and tangible actions. When setting clear expectations, consolidation helps the individual identify what is most important and where their energy should be directed. When setting clear expectations, consolidation saves leaders from a trap that often derails even the noblest of efforts. This trap many leaders fall victim to is a tendency to overextend their direct reports by providing too many goals or objectives. Providing too many goals or objectives easily overwhelms even the most seasoned individuals and often results in their failure to meet expectations. When consolidating, an ideal or target number of action items should range anywhere from 3-5 items.

After facilitating self-reliant problem solving and collaborating on our path forward, Andrew and I worked together to identify the 3-5 most critical items he needed to address. Then, he articulated his next steps and I asked that he document our plan by sending it to me via email. Asking Andrew to articulate our plan and to follow-up in writing was critical because it served as a performance agreement between us. Also, it served as a tangible item that provided transparency on our next steps. Before concluding the meeting, I asked Andrew to include my role in his plan and what he needed from me for it to be a success. At the end of our meeting, I asked Andrew for a final recap of everything we discussed. He provided a thorough explanation and ensured me he was 100% committed to the next steps.

For Andrew, the next steps were not easy. In fact, in the following weeks, Andrew took it upon himself to schedule some very difficult meetings with both his direct reports and key stakeholders. Individuals who attended these meetings informed me that Andrew spoke candidly about his opportunities for development and took full ownership for his previous lack of leadership. Additionally, it was shared with me that during these meetings Andrew directly stated, "I vow to do better" and asked others to hold him accountable for the execution of his plan which included specific behaviors that he intended to address immediately. In probing to gain a little more insight on these "specific behaviors", I was pleased to hear that Andrew shared his list of 3-5 critical behaviors he needed to address and asked for their partnership in ensuring that he gets better. Andrew shared that their feedback would be vital to his plan and encouraged open dialogue.

By proactively scheduling these meetings and taking ownership of his previous inefficiencies, Andrew started the process of righting his wrongs, showed an immense amount of vulnerability, and ultimately built trust within his team and key stakeholders. What's more impressive is that this action was not mandated by me. Yet, it clearly illustrated that Andrew was completely sold on our plan. Over the next three months, Andrew carefully executed the plan and began reconstructing his reputation as a leader. In reflecting on the time spent with Andrew and his timely transformation, it is clear that Andrew experienced tremendous growth. The impact of Andrew's growth was evident by the fact that his direct reports and key stakeholders began to see him in a different light. Some specific comments shared with me were: "I don't know what has gotten into Andrew, but I like it." and "Andrew is much more focused on driving results through action. What did you do to him?" Ironically, the truth is, I did not do anything TO him. Instead, I simply *trusted the process* and worked in partnership WITH him to set clear expectations.

In its entirety, the transformational conversation between Andrew and I did not last more than 30 minutes. However, throughout those 30 minutes, I needed to trust the process and execute accordingly. In this instance, execution involved setting clear expectations through the careful implementation of our Critical Five Leadership Competencies: Candor, Calibration, Clarification, Collaboration, and Consolidation (C5LC). In illustrating this approach, Andrew's story highlights that in the early stages of our conversation, he was acting like a "poor sailor who blames the wind." Yet, by the conclusion, it was evident that he was ready to harness the wind's energy and chart a new course.

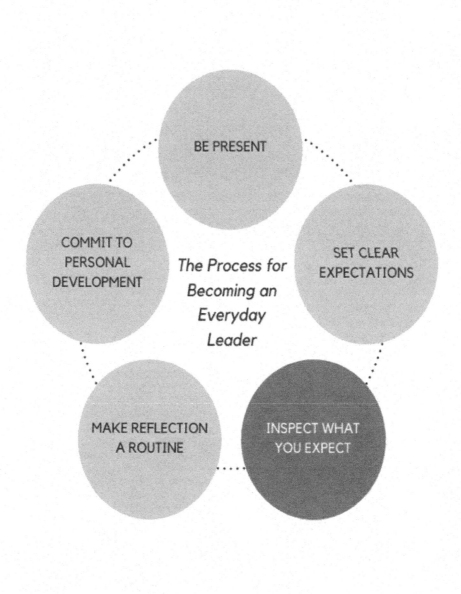

BE PRESENT

COMMIT TO
PERSONAL
DEVELOPMENT

*The Process for
Becoming an
Everyday
Leader*

SET CLEAR
EXPECTATIONS

MAKE REFLECTION
A ROUTINE

INSPECT WHAT
YOU EXPECT

CHAPTER 3: INSPECT WHAT YOU EXPECT

"What gets measured, gets done."

~Peter Drucker

A s a lover of food and traveling, I often rely heavily on my GPS to take me exactly where I want to go. It doesn't matter if I am venturing out to a new restaurant or taking a road trip across the country, my GPS is a useful tool for both guidance and direction. Without it, there is a high probability that I could end up lost even in my city of residence. With that in mind, take a moment to reflect on a time when you used a GPS:

- What was your destination?

- How did the GPS assist you in getting to your destination?

- How frequently did you change course?

- What led to you either changing course or staying course?

- How often did you check the time, distance, traffic, and/or tolls?

In reflecting on the above questions, you may already be drawing parallels between using a GPS to track progress toward your destination and the equally important aspect of **inspecting** progress toward your **expected** personal and professional goal(s). Imagine putting an unfamiliar destination into your GPS and then blindly moving forward without ever referring to the map for direction. If you are like most people, the thought of this probably seems crazy. Yet, at home and in the workplace, we often set lofty goals and blindly move forward without ever **inspecting** our progress. Simply put, setting clear expectations and goals is critical to the process of becoming an everyday leader. Still, installing the proper controls to inspect progression toward said expectations is an equally vital part of the process. Accordingly, this chapter will spotlight how to effectively *Inspect What You Expect* because we believe that failure to do so will inevitably result in a lack of alignment, accountability, and productivity.

An important note, when reviewing the remainder of this chapter, be advised Inspecting What You Expect is *not*, I repeat NOT, an excuse to over-supervise or micromanage. Over-supervising and/or micromanaging are direct indicators that there is an absence of trust. And when trust is absent, the outcome is often a decrease in efficiency, productivity, and engagement. Trust is one soft skill that has a proven hard impact. Thus, a critical distinction to make is that, when Inspecting What You Expect, the approach must encapsulate positive intentions and not result in over-supervising or micromanaging.

Meet Amanda

To further emphasize the importance of Inspecting What You Expect, we introduce the real-life character of Amanda and her journey to understanding. Having over 20 years of industry experience, Amanda served as Senior Director for a large matrixed organization. Her role included overseeing critical aspects of professional development for managers and individual contributors across the enterprise. Amanda was well-liked and respected by nearly everyone in the organization, including her direct reports which consisted of 8-10 supervisors. Over the years, Amanda developed a strong reputation for building relationships and driving results; it is to this point that the next portion of the story was so troubling for her.

As part of Amanda's role, she was expected to oversee the work of her direct reports and ensure that they develop into better leaders. With most of her direct reports, Amanda was extremely successful in meeting or exceeding these expectations. However, Amanda had one direct report, Trevor, who consistently missed deadlines, failed to hit expected metrics, and did not seem to be progressing appropriately. When it came to Trevor, Amanda was near her wits' end. The most recent instance of Trevor failing to meet expected metrics emerged at the end of the month when he totaled a mere 8 out of the 40 expected coaching sessions. The problem here was that Amanda knew coaching sessions were a critical component for developing associates and had previously shared this sentiment with all of her direct reports, including Trevor. Additionally, Amanda had previously expressed to her direct reports that if coaching sessions were not occurring, she assumed that associates were not receiving the development needed to improve their craft. Trevor's failure to execute these expectations, for the third consecutive month, resulted in Amanda being livid.

To gain better insight and understanding as to what went wrong, Amanda carefully reviewed the coaching report which displayed a summary of the sessions logged by each of her direct reports. After thoroughly reviewing the report, Amanda picked up the phone and called Trevor. Remembering her training and avoiding the trap of letting her emotions overtake her actions, Amanda started the conversation by tactfully, yet candidly, expressing her concern. After being transparent about her extreme disappointment, Amanda opened the lines of communication and allowed Trevor an opportunity to explain. Throughout Trevor's explanation, Amanda practiced being fully present and maintained laser-focus on her intent to gain a better understanding of the problem.

After gaining a more thorough understanding of the problem, Amanda realized that Trevor felt overwhelmed and completely lost about how to accomplish 40 coaching sessions while still balancing other critical expectations of the role. It was at this point that Amanda **reflected on the process** (a step-by-step approach to reflection that will be unveiled in the next chapter), realized her shortcomings as a leader, and decided to develop a new plan to better assist her direct report. Through reflection, Amanda realized the initial plan did not include enough touchpoints throughout the month to measure and ensure progress toward the stated goal. Consequently, by the end of the month, it was far too late for Trevor to receive valuable and timely feedback. Essentially, Amanda realized that by failing to encompass an adequate number of touchpoints within the initial plan, she was unintentionally sending Trevor to a foreign destination while refusing to provide him with the much-needed guidance and direction of a GPS.

To combat this problem, Amanda quickly collaborated with Trevor to revise their initial plan and set more clearly defined expectations. The result of this collaboration was a new and improved plan which consisted of weekly touchpoint meetings and entailed a minimum goal of 10 coaching sessions per week. Amanda and Trevor both agreed that if 10 coaching sessions were not completed by the end of each week, being agile enough to make changes on the fly would be essential to ensuring success. Trevor agreed that he should be responsible for making the necessary adjustments since he is the one who would be closest to the action. As a result, contingency plans were made and an agreement was established, that failure to course correct or adapt to change was simply not an option. Finally, as part of the plan, Amanda communicated to Trevor, "If for any reason you feel that you will not be able to meet our agreed upon goal of 10 coaching sessions per week, please let me know immediately." Trevor nodded in agreement and shared that he would provide a weekly update during their weekly touchpoint meetings.

At this point, Amanda and Trevor both bought into the plan and were eager to begin execution. Of equal importance, the new plan resulted in increased alignment, accountability, and empowerment. Fast forward thirty days, and the coaching sessions report was again distributed to all leaders. Surprisingly, Amanda felt no need to review Trevor's total number of coaching sessions completed for the month, which was only the case because, through their weekly touchpoint meetings, Amanda was already informed that 53 coaching sessions were completed within the month. Nonetheless, Amanda reviewed the report and was proud of what she saw. Accordingly, Amanda took a moment to celebrate Trevor's success by picking up the phone and calling him to extend a heartfelt congratulations on a successful month. Trevor thanked Amanda for the patience and direction provided. Additionally, he went on to reassure Amanda that this effort and outcome would become the new normal.

In the story shared at the onset of this chapter, Amanda's initial failures threatened to derail the success of both her and Trevor. It would have been easy for Amanda to take the position that Trevor should have contacted her the moment he began to feel overwhelmed. However, as a reputable leader within her company, Amanda personified what it means to become an everyday leader, focusing on what she could control and how she could play a role in resolving the issue at hand. Through years of experience, Amanda knew playing the blame game would have resulted in Trevor becoming defensive, shutting down, and decreasing productivity. Thus, in avoiding the trap to partake in the blame game, Amanda demonstrated complete ownership of the situation by acknowledging her shortcomings as a leader. This rarely seen level of vulnerability from a leader allowed Trevor to feel at ease and more willing to create and execute a superior plan.

Throughout this story, Amanda demonstrated a willingness to be present. She also showed clear expectations are useless without the proper systems in place to monitor and inspect said expectations. Amanda's initial failure highlighted the importance of reflecting on the process and, through demonstrated introspection, she was able to be vulnerable, admit her faults, and collaborate with Trevor to modify their initial plan. This resulted in a new and improved plan with clearer expectations and checkpoints to ensure progression toward said expectations. It was to this end that Amanda empowered Trevor to exceed his goal of 40 coaching sessions per month, and displayed why she is viewed as one of the most effective leaders within her organization. In practice, inspecting does not have to be a "formal" process, and the frequency of "inspections" will vary based on the nature of the task at hand and the competence of the individual. But, let's be clear, if you want to ensure success, consistently inspecting what you expect has to be a part of the process. In other words, if it is important and you want to see it completed, remember Drucker's words: "What gets measured, gets done."

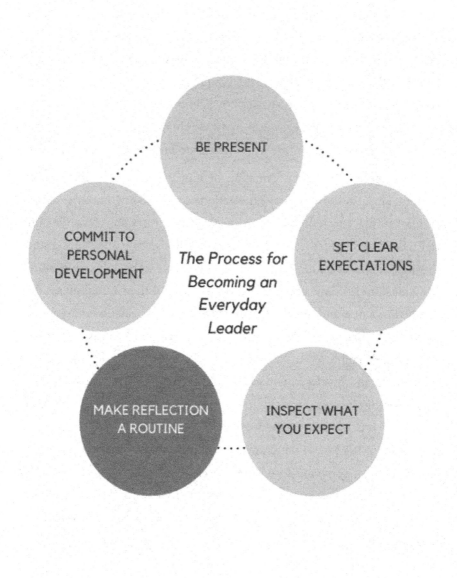

CHAPTER 4: MAKE REFLECTION A ROUTINE

"There is one art of which people should
be masters – the art of reflection."
– Samuel Taylor Coleridge

A s a professor of education, much of my role entails teaching, coaching, mentoring, and training future school teachers. And, through experience, I have come to realize most people do not grasp the amount of work it takes to become a teacher. The systematic learning and training process that future teachers must endure encapsulates:

- The four-year degree (two years of general education and two years in teacher candidacy)

- Up to 100 hours of early field experiences which include on-the-job learning in public school classrooms through observations, clinicals, and practicum placements

- Up to 640 hours of full-time student teaching

- Successful completion of the teacher performance assessment portfolio and

- Passing a state mandated licensing examination

Without successful completion of each component, one cannot become a licensed teacher. Consequently, even some of my most well-prepared future teachers succumb to the pressure of unforeseen challenges in the classroom and often reach out to me for guidance. One specific instance of this occurred during a routine one-on-one meeting with a beginning teacher, Tessa.

Tessa approached me to discuss a lesson plan that she was preparing for her high school students. She was extremely excited about the plan and looking forward to delivering it. During our meeting, she detailed every step of her lesson plan that would ultimately result in students creating a marketing campaign for a local company. Surprisingly, Tessa had already contacted the company and coordinated with representatives to have them join the classroom and serve as judges during student pitches. Tessa could hardly contain her excitement while sharing that she had created a three week-long strategy to help students master the content and produce their final products. I was extremely excited for Tessa and completely present throughout our conversation. Before the conclusion of our one-on-one meeting, I set the expectation with Tessa that I wanted to hear back from her within a week because I was eager to hear how things were progressing. At the end of the first week, I received a call from Tessa. Still excited for her, I eagerly asked, "What's on your mind?" and "How are things going?" Instantly, I could tell her tone was different. She said:

- The students are not as excited as I thought they would be.

- Only about 60% of the class passed the first quiz assessing their mastery of the content.

- I am not sure if they are ready for next week considering they are supposed to start on their projects soon.

- I have to figure out what I can do better by Monday for my students.

For me, this last sentiment was the one that resonated most loudly, so I'll repeat it, "I have to figure out what I can do better by Monday for my students." This statement was music to my ears because it demonstrated a willingness to learn and emphasized the importance of reflection. Reflection is a critical process necessary for leaders to continually develop and can be sparked through critical questions such as:

- How can I improve?

- Did we reach the desired outcomes of our work?

- What can I do differently next time?

- What made this project such a success (or failure)?

These are merely a few examples of critical questions that can be asked for reflective purposes. This chapter provides an overview of the critical role reflection plays in the process of becoming an everyday leader, and a detailed strategy to help you make reflection a routine in your work.

Reflection

Reflection, in my experience, has been a word thrown around as if people are just expected to know what it means. The truth is, for the most part, everyone does know what reflection means (to give serious thought to something; contemplation). However, what is usually missing from the conversation on reflection is 1) what makes it important and 2) how it is done.

To answer the first question, reflection is important because it supports professional and personal development. Taking time to ask what happened and why often pushes people to operate differently.

In the book *Reach, Touch, Teach*, Terry Borton created a model for reflection called "What, So What, Now What," as a sequence. This model requires one to ask the *what* questions to review the events (e.g., "What happened?"), the *so what* questions to analyze the events (e.g., "So what were the outcomes?"), and finally, the *now what* questions as a way to move forward (e.g., "Now what do I need to do as a result?"). We like the simplicity of Borton's model and offer you an extension designed to complement this sequence. We call it the "R.E.C.I.T.E." approach.

R.E.C.I.T.E. is an acronym that combines the necessary actions and required mindset for practicing reflection: *Recall, Evaluate, Celebrate, Intentional, Timely,* and *Emphasize.* To recite something, by definition, means to repeat something from memory. Because reflection largely occurs after an action has taken place, R.E.C.I.T.E. is a fitting approach. In the section that follows, each component of the acronym is explained in greater detail.

Recall

The first step is to *recall* the details of the day, event, or situation back to remembrance. The process of reflection requires you to mentally return to the "place" you want to examine. Key questions to ask yourself include:

- What was the sequence of events?

- What was the original goal?

- Who was involved?

In the scenario with Tessa, during our phone conversation, which occurred after the lessons, she was able to recall all of her original student outcomes. From there, she then tried to pinpoint what went wrong. This led to the need for *evaluation*.

Evaluate

The evaluation phase is all about intentionally setting aside time to measure the successes and/or failures related to your day, event, or situation. As you recall the details of the day, situation, or event, be sure to review your target outcomes. Whether or not you met or missed your goal(s), dig deeper to figure out why. Being introspective and using a critical lens will allow you to expand your reflections beyond simply recalling what happened, leading to a much deeper level of understanding. To reach this deeper level of understanding, we propose learning and practicing the art of metacognition. In layman's terms, metacognition is a skill that entails being aware of and understanding your thought processes. Throughout our conversation, Tessa drilled deeper, focusing on what worked and what didn't work. She reviewed her lessons, questioned weaknesses in her anticipatory set (how teachers launch lessons), and critiqued her lesson plans. Her exact words were, "Maybe my launch missed the mark needed to garner student excitement." Additionally, because there was evidence that indicated a lack of content mastery, she expressed: "My lessons did not include enough checkpoints to ensure understanding throughout delivery."

Essentially, from her evaluation, Tessa realized that she did not quite *inspect her expectations* throughout the duration of the teaching/learning segment. Using this example, we see Tessa evaluating her lessons to provide a more thorough assessment of her situation. It was important, however, that Tessa be reminded that not all was a complete failure and there were some moments to celebrate.

Celebrate

Sometimes in the reflection process people focus more on what went wrong and how to improve, while neglecting what went right. While celebrating your successes is a key component of reflective practice, many people tend to overlook its importance. Hence, we urge you to celebrate your wins, both big and small. To accomplish this, you must first recognize your wins as both credible and legitimate victories. In a 2015 Inc. article, Carmody wrote about the psychological effects of celebrating accomplishments, saying, "If you fail to celebrate your many accomplishments, you are training your brain that what you are doing isn't all that exciting and important." Accordingly, during this stage of the reflection process, we propose asking yourself questions such as:

- What went well?

- How did I win?

- What did I learn?

- Who did I help?

- How did I help?

- What was my impact?

From the previous section, it may appear that Tessa did not set aside time to celebrate her successes. However, that was not the case. During our phone call, I asked Tessa to review her student scores. She noted, "Only about 60% of the class passed the first quiz assessing their mastery of the content." When Tessa reviewed the scores, she realized most of her students only missed the mark by a couple of points (for many teachers, mastery can

39

reflect a score of 85%). In light of this new revelation, I asked Tessa, "Is that not enough to provide some relief?" By pointing out that the remediation needed should be relatively easy considering how close to the mark her students were, I was able to talk Tessa off the ledge. Additionally, Tessa needed to be reminded that the partnership she scored for her students was a major win. Tessa then admitted that, when she mentioned the project details to her students, they were immensely excited. In turn, I told her that sounded like a win and she needed to celebrate!

Up until this point, we have reviewed the first half of the R.E.C.I.T.E. (R.E.C) which is all about the practice of reflection. The following components (I. T. E.) are less about *how to practice reflection*, but more about *the mindset needed for successful reflection*. Let's begin by learning more about the need for intentionality.

Intentional

By definition, being *intentional* means to be deliberate and purposeful. Reflection should not be approached simply because it is demanded or expected of you. You must set an intention to be reflective of your practice for the benefits it brings you and your development. Without intention, reflections are likely to remain surface level and, in turn, less likely to promote the change it is capable of manifesting. Tessa's reflection epitomizes intentionality because she saw the need for it and ignited the process on her own. Taking time to sit with and process the events allowed her to proceed in a way that was more deliberate and purposeful. In addition to her intentionality, Tessa began to engage in the process of reflection in a timely manner.

Timely

Memory is fleeting and because reflection relies on our ability to recall facts, timeliness is essential. Reflection should happen as soon as possible. To properly reflect, you must be in the right mental space to reflect and if you are not ready, wait until it is the appropriate time. But, make every effort to reflect as soon as possible. For some, this is the end of the workday;

for others, it is the next day, or it can be the end of the workweek. The time-liness factor involves how soon you can participate in the reflection process to ensure proper memory recall, but also requires you to be mentally present for the work of reflection. You must find your groove. My moments of reflection happen most often during long drives to and from work. At this time, I intentionally turn down the radio and make time to recall, evaluate, and celebrate aspects of my day. From the example with Tessa, we see her reach the end of a school week and know that she says, "I have to figure out what I can do better by Monday for my students." The immediacy of Tessa's reflection is rooted in the fact that she has to recourse rather quickly. While this timeline may not be true for you in your situation, it is still imperative that you remember: the longer you wait to engage in reflection, the more muddled the details will become. Besides, the longer you wait, the power of reflection itself dwindles because the goal is to use what is uncovered to shape how you navigate moving forward. Here, Tessa not only realized the need to be timely in her reflection, but she also emphasized it.

Emphasize

As it relates to mindset, this last component emphasizes the necessity of reflection. If you research the definition of *emphasize*, you are going to find something like, "give special importance to" or "lay stress on." Reflection in your work should be a critical component; you will need to give special importance to the power of reflection and stress the need for growth in the process. From our example, we see Tessa, a brand-new classroom teacher, engage in reflection. As a trained educator and a teacher educator, I too constantly engage in reflection and would admonish you to adopt a mindset of emphasizing reflection to facilitate the process of becoming an everyday leader.

Cooperative Reflection

While becoming a reflective practitioner is often deemed to be solo work, it should also happen cooperatively when needed. Case in point: What did Tessa do? She called her mentor to receive some support during the process. This is a clear-cut example of engaging in cooperative reflection. First, she reflected in isolation, then called in her reinforcements. In Corporate America, rotational leadership programs are all the rave because they offer valuable insight and perspective to emerging leaders. These leaders are often paired with mentors inside their organization so that they can learn and share best practices with one another. In the world of education, we use a similar strategy known as peer observations to improve our practice. My peers have been able to, as somewhat of an outsider to my classrooms, offer me differing perspectives. These perspectives and insights are then included in my journaling and private reflection time. This is an example of layered cooperative reflection: layer one - I reflect individually, layer two - I meet with others for cooperative reflection, and layer three - I reconvene individual reflection through journaling.

In your work, how can others play a role in your reflection process?

Let's look to a national summer literacy program, Freedom School, for another example.

A required component of the work staff members complete during the summer is called "daily debrief." This is a time at the end of a workday when staff is required to come together as a team to process their day, discuss successes and challenges, review logistics, and prepare for the day ahead. Daily debrief, whether fifteen minutes or one hour long, is rooted in the need for reflection. Freedom School, as an organization, created a culture in which reflection is important. We offer you this example for two reasons: 1) to show you a simple approach and 2) to ask, have you created a culture of reflective practice (at home, at work, with your team, within yourself, etc.)?

Pete Hall and Alisa Simeral's book *Creating a Culture of Reflective Practice: Building Capacity for Schoolwide Success* offers an operational definition of a culture of reflective practice:

> a culture of reflective practice is an organization that embraces reflective growth as the primary driving force behind continuous,

lasting improvement. In such an organization, members speak the language of reflection, engage in rigorous metacognitive tasks, and earnestly support their individual and collective growth. The entire organization oozes self-reflection.

Does your team and organization "ooze" self-reflection? If not, what will it take to get them there? From our experience, to ignite a culture of reflection, we recommend asking four questions at the end of every project. Those questions are:

- What went well?

- What didn't go so well?

- What have we learned?

- What still puzzles us?[1]

To conclude, while the references here were originally intended for educators, we argue that being a reflective practitioner is crucial, regardless of profession or position. With this in mind, we urge you to challenge yourself to make reflection a routine. We believe reflection changes you. It changes your perspectives. It changes your action. It charts a new course for the days ahead. Thorough reflection can help you repeat successes and avoid duplicating failures. As you seek to grow and develop as a leader, reflection is a mandatory component. After all, Coleridge did say, *"There is one art of which people should be masters – the art of reflection."*

---

1 *Note: These questions are also appropriate for individual reflection.*

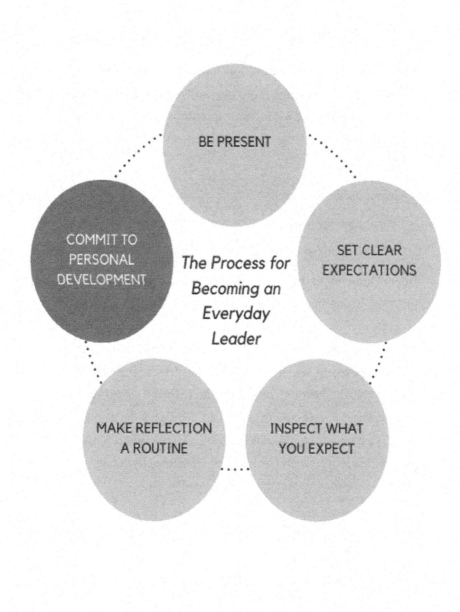

BE PRESENT

COMMIT TO PERSONAL DEVELOPMENT

The Process for Becoming an Everyday Leader

SET CLEAR EXPECTATIONS

MAKE REFLECTION A ROUTINE

INSPECT WHAT YOU EXPECT

CHAPTER 5: COMMIT TO PERSONAL DEVELOPMENT

"Those who cannot change their minds cannot change anything."
~ George Bernard Shaw

It may come as no surprise that the final chapter of this book focuses on *personal development*, or personal leadership. In the preceding sections, we provided you with what we believe are essential components for leadership development. Oftentimes, we think about leadership as a skill we have to strengthen solely so that others can reap the benefits. However, we would argue that personal development should be your first priority. As you work to make yourself better, you will in turn become a better leader, and the people you serve will benefit.

We define personal leadership as the process of inspiring and guiding self-improvement. Extending on our definition of leadership provided earlier in the book (an outcome-based process in which an individual intentionally opts to exert direct or indirect influence over another individual or group of individuals), when you exercise personal leadership, you exert direct influence over yourself. This chapter provides four suggestions for refining and advancing your personal leadership. Additionally, this section of the book is designed to be more interactive, so we have provided a workspace for you to capture notes.

1. **Write a personal vision and mission statement.**

According to Bain & Company, "a vision statement describes the desired future position of the company." It is okay if you are a little idealistic here because if you put in the work, those ideals can be achieved, correct? Take a look at a few examples of vision statements from notable organizations:

- Alzheimer's Association: "A world without Alzheimer's disease."

- Amazon: "To be Earth's most customer-centric company, where customers can find and discover anything they might want to buy online."

- Nike: "To remain the most authentic, connected, and distinctive brand."

- Teach for America: "One day, all children in this nation will have the opportunity to attain an excellent education."

The vision statement should be more future-oriented. One way to think about this is to liken it to the way that people approach vision boards. Often, at the start of the new year, people break out magazines and other arts and crafts supplies to find representation for the goals they would like to achieve. A similar approach can be applied to writing your vision statement.

Take a moment to think about the questions below which will help you craft your personal vision statement.

- What three wishes would you make if you had a genie in a bottle?

- What is your biggest dream or goal in life?

- What have you always loved doing?

- What are you really good at?

- What is the legacy you want to leave behind?

Prepare a **rough draft** of your vision statement here:

_____

_____

_____

_____

_____

_____

Referring again to Bain & Company: "A mission statement defines the company's business, its objectives and its approach to reach those objectives." Let's look at a few companies and their mission statements:

- Amazon: "To be Earth's most customer-centric company, where customers can find and discover anything they might want to buy online, and endeavors to offer its customers the lowest possible prices."

- Nike: "To bring inspiration and innovation to every athlete in the world."

- Twitter: "To give people the power to share and make the world more open and connected."

We think you would agree that these companies certainly strive to make their mission a reality; it drives the work they do. Essentially, it is the work of the mission that makes the vision a reality. Using this definition and the examples, create a mission statement focusing solely on your personal development. The mission should be related to your professional and personal aspirations.

Take a moment to think about the questions below that can help you craft your personal mission statement.

- What are you most passionate about?

- Who do you wish to serve?

- How do you intend to be of service to others?

- What unique talents do you bring to the table?

Prepare a **rough draft** of your mission statement here:

_____

_____

_____

_____

_____

_____

Before creating your final drafts, identify an accountability partner to review your rough drafts. This accountability partner should be a trusted source who will provide you with candid feedback and hold you accountable for keeping your commitment. Through this process of cooperative reflection, make edits to your rough drafts.

Insert a **revision** of your vision statement here:

_____

_____

_____

_____

_____

_____

Insert a **revision** of your mission statement here:

_____

_____

_____

_____

_____

On a final note, we were first introduced to writing personal mission statements via the critically acclaimed *7 Habits of Highly Effective People* by Stephen Covey. A few of his statements ring so true for this process that they are worth repeating here:

- "A mission statement is not something you write overnight."
- "It becomes the criterion by which you measure everything else in your life."
- "I find the process is as important as the product. Writing or reviewing a mission statement changes you because it forces you

to think through your priorities deeply, carefully, and to align your behavior with your beliefs."

So now that you have completed your first and second iterations of a vision and mission statement, recognize that refining these statements is a process. We urge you to consider how the process will ensure alignment between your work and your beliefs.

2. **Engage in ongoing goal setting.**

While your vision and mission statements serve to undergird your personal development process, it is also recommended that you are setting and updating personal goals regularly. To accomplish this, we endorse the SMART and SMARTER goal-setting frameworks. The SMART goal framework is well-known and cited throughout professional literature. The acronym is used broadly and is widely accepted but the verbiage can vary. Regardless, the SMART goals "formula" operates as a guide to support goal setters by identifying the following:

- **Specific:** This requires you to be clear and straightforward in articulating the goal. Ask yourself: Is my goal specific? For example-

  o *I want to lose weight* vs. *I want to lose 10 pounds.* The latter goal here is more specific.

- **Measurable:** This component asks you to determine how your goal, or progress toward the goal, can be gauged. You will need to identify a way to quantify the goal so there is evidence that you are making progress. Ask yourself: Can progression toward my goal be measured? For example-

  o *I will track the progress of my weight loss by weighing in two times a week.*

- **Actionable:** Identify clear steps that can be taken to achieve the goal. Ask yourself: What are the clear steps I can take to achieve my goal? For example-

  o *I will achieve this by meal prepping on Sundays and working out 2-3 times a week.*

- **Realistic/Relevant:** Determine how the goal is aligned to other aspects of your work, life, and desires and if it can be achieved as articulated. Ask yourself: Is my goal realistic and am I motivated to achieve it? For example-

  o *I know losing a few pounds will positively impact my health and well-being.*

- **Time-related:** Have you ever heard the saying, "A goal that is not written down is merely a wish?" This framework not only forces you to write down the goal, but also requires you to specify when the goal should be met. Ask yourself: Is there a clear or definitive timeline for which this goal must be achieved? For example-

  o *I will lose (at least) the first five pounds within three weeks.*

According to Duncan Haughey, the SMART goal framework has been extended to a SMARTER goals framework, adding:

- **Evaluated:** Evaluating goals requires completing an appraisal of the goal to determine the extent to which it has been achieved. Ask yourself: Where the outcomes of your goal met? For example-

  o *Three weeks passed and in terms of progress and actually losing this weight, I have lost 6 lbs.*

- **Reviewed:** To review your goals, you have to reflect and make an adjustment to your approach or behavior to reach the goal. Ask yourself: What adjustments need to be made? What are your next steps? For example-o   *Based on my evaluation, I know I still have 4 lbs to lose. to do so, I will implement a new technique: intermittent fasting.*

In the scenario above, we provide you with a personal example using the SMARTER goal framework. Using this blueprint, craft a SMARTER goal for yourself as it relates to your leadership development.

S: *What do you want to accomplish?* **Be specific.**

_____

M: *What can you do to track and monitor your progress?* **Provide a metric.**

_____

A: *What steps will you take to achieve this goal?* **Outline exactly what you will do.**

_____

R: *Why this goal? How does it align with my life?* **Describe your motivation and its relevance.**

_____

T: *What is the realistic time frame for accomplishing this goal?* **Provide a specific date.**

_____

E: *Given the time that has passed, what is the status of the goal?* **Practice the R.E.C.I.T.E. approach.**

_____

R: *Based on the status of your goal, what are my next steps?* **Ensure alignment between the next steps and your goal, mission, and vision.**

_____

As you may have realized, when it is time for you to evaluate and review the goal, you will find yourself back at the beginning of the goal framework writing a new goal.

3. **Enter the garden of personal development.**

If you talk to any serious gardener, they will likely share some key gems for getting started with your garden, such as: understand the seasons, care for the plants to avoid pests, and make sure they have the proper nutrients.proper nutrients.We were drawn to the garden analogy after reading John Brandon's article called "*6 Ways Great Leadership Is Exactly Like Gardening.*" Using this same garden analogy in a different way, ask yourself the following:

- What season are you in right now professionally (and personally), and what season is coming next?

- How do these seasons, and your needs, vary from one another?

- What habits or attitudes are you currently struggling with that could be likened to a "pest?"

- How do you alter unfavorable behaviors to grow?

- What support (i.e. plant nutrients) do you need to seek out and secure?

- How might an external coach assist with your personal development?

While this list of questions is not all-encompassing, it can serve as a starting point to help you cultivate your "garden." In this case, you are both the garden and gardener. Thus, you must develop your "green thumb."

4. **Trust the Process:**

As discussed in the previous chapter, the process of reflection is ongoing. Accordingly, we advocate that leaders self-assess using each piece of the framework we have presented.

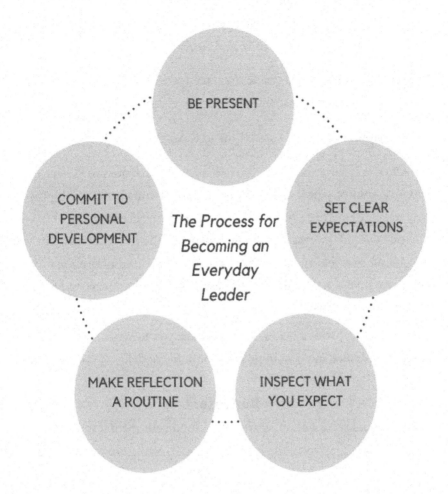

The framework is represented cyclically because it never actually ends. In implementing the process of becoming an everyday leader, you may move from one step of the model to the next, but being a good leader means exercising positive intent. And, to exercise positive intent you should always strive to be better tomorrow than you are today. To accomplish this, you must always ask yourself:

1. How present am I in my everyday interactions with colleagues, friends, and family?

2. How would my colleagues, friends, and family describe the clarity of my expectations for them?

3. How frequently and effectively am I inspecting my expectations of my colleagues, friends, and family?

4. How often do I set aside time to engage in reflection on my work, projects, and personal/professional relationships?

5. How often do I set aside time to water my garden?

Once you have taken the time to answer these questions, you enter the final step of personal development and essentially start the process over again. Remember, this framework is both a process and an outcome. The outcome of addressing all components of the model is that you will become a better leader. However, be cautious and mindful that the process entails no final arrival. Good leaders adopt a growth mindset and practice continuous self-improvement.

In the spaces provided below, we encourage you to write notes using the prompts provided in effort to practice with the model.

Be Present

Take away distractions and worries that cloud your mental space. Answer:

What can I do to be more present in "the moment"?

Set Clear Expectations and Boundaries

In this work, we must monitor how we communicate our expectations to avoid confusion and disappointment. Answer:

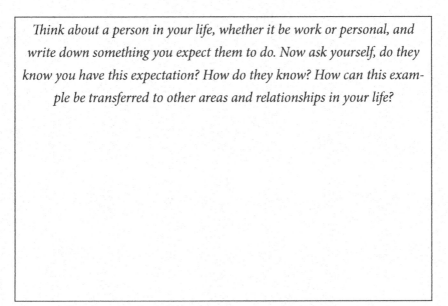

Think about a person in your life, whether it be work or personal, and write down something you expect them to do. Now ask yourself, do they know you have this expectation? How do they know? How can this example be transferred to other areas and relationships in your life?

Inspect What You Expect

Inspecting your progression toward your expectations and goals is vital. Answer:

What are some standard approaches I can adopt/implement to assess my progression toward my goals or expectations of myself and others?

Reflect on the Process

Thorough reflection can help you repeat successes and avoid repeating failures. Answer:

> *What does reflection look like for me? How can I be more intentional about reflection in my work and life in general? How can I include others in this process?*

Commit to Personal Development

Like a garden, I require some tilling. Answer:

> *What areas of my work (or life) need more finetuning? What could that look like?*

Essentially, you have to be capable of leading yourself before you can effectively lead others. This process of personal development will make you better. As a result, those you serve will benefit as well. In addition to (1) writing personal vision and mission statements, (2) engaging in SMARTER goal setting, (3) cultivating your garden, and (4) trusting the process, we also encourage you to think about and develop areas of your life that you know need work and can make you a much better leader. For some, these areas may include self-confidence, time management, organization, and self-discipline. After all, you have to be able to change yourself first before changing anything else.

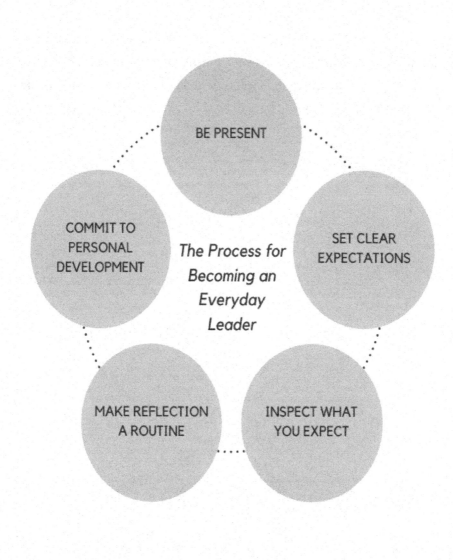

CONCLUSION

At the onset of this book, we shared that our quintessential goal was to ensure you gain a better understanding of how to become a more effective leader. To accomplish said goal, we (1) provided a clear definition of leadership, (2) described what it means to be an everyday leader, (3) distinguished good leadership from bad leadership, and (4) unveiled a practical five-step model to becoming an everyday leader. As a recap, you may recall that our definition of leadership can be summed up as an outcome-based process in which an individual intentionally opts to exert direct or indirect influence over another individual or group of individuals. By defining leadership in this manner, it becomes a learnable and teachable skill that can improve through the intentionality of ongoing and sustained practice.

Further, we emphasized our belief that everyone is a leader and/or possesses leadership capabilities. To explain, we highlighted and defined everyday leadership as ownership of one's inherent capability to influence self and others. Next, we juxtaposed good leadership and bad leadership. In attempting to make a clear distinction between the two, we proposed that good leadership produces a positive outcome and is the result of positive intentions. Whereas, bad leadership may produce a positive or negative outcome and be the result of positive or negative intentions. Simply put, in the results-driven world that we live in, if you cannot produce positive outcomes, you cannot call yourself a good leader; and, with a heightened sense of attention being placed on ethical leadership, if you do not display positive intent, you cannot call yourself a good leader.

Lastly, in unveiling our model to becoming an everyday leader, we leveraged personal stories and experiences to spotlight five critical steps which are: *Be Present, Set Clear Expectations, Inspect What You Expect, Reflect on the Process, and Commit to Personal Development.* In reminiscing on our personal stories, we hope they serve as a reminder for you to *Trust the Process.* As illustrated, trusting the process will look different for each individual. In some instances, trusting the process may require you to be present like the department chair. In other instances like Andrew's, it may require you to set clear expectations using the Critical 5 Leadership Competencies of Candor, Calibration, Clarification, Collaboration, and Consolidation. Still, there may be other instances where it is imperative to adhere to the lessons learned by Amanda and carefully inspect what you expect. All the while, threaded within each of the above stories, and that of Tessa's, is the crucial need to reflect on the process and commit to personal development. This need serves as the perfect segue for our call to action.

CALL TO ACTION

As trained educators and leaders operating in both formal and informal leadership roles, we strive daily to personify what it means to become an everyday leader. Yet, through reflection, it is blatantly obvious that our quest to become the optimal leader is a never-ending one. Consequently, we spend every day of our lives, at home and work, trusting the process and intentionally working to become a better leader. It is to this point that we ask you to join us in our quest to become the best leaders imaginable. To achieve this, we recommend you trust the process and share what you have learned with those closest to you. Consider spending a week or month at a time focusing solely on improving one aspect of the five-step model to becoming an everyday leader. Perhaps you accomplish this by taking the information learned back to your work team, loved ones, friends, or associates and, together, create a commitment to hold one another accountable for becoming an everyday leader. Research suggests (and our personal experiences would support) that the best way to master a new skill is to try teaching it to someone else. Thus, if you truly trust and want to master the process: who will you teach first, and when will you begin?

NOTES

Introduction

John Maxwell, *The 21 Irrefutable Laws of Leadership*

Simon Sinek, *Start with Why*

Peter Northouse, Professor Emeritus of Communication, Western Michigan University https://us.sagepub.com/en-us/nam/northouseauthor

Ho, M. (2017). *Learning investment and hours are on the rise* Retrieved from https://www.td.org/magazines/td-magazine/ learning-investment-and-hours-are-on-the-rise

Chapter 2

John Miller, *QBQ! The Question Behind The Question*

Kim Scott, *Radical Candor: Be a Kick-Ass Boss Without Losing Your Humanity*

Julie Zhuo, *The Making of a Manager*

Gardner, H. & Ibarra, H. (2017). How to capture value from collaboration, especially If you're skeptical about it. Retrieved from https:// hbr.org/2017/05/how-to-capture-value-from-collaboration-especially-if-youre-skeptical-about-it

Harvard Business Review. (2019). Meeting the challenges of developing collaborative teams for future success. Retrieved from https://hbr.org/sponsored/2019/09/

meeting-the-challenges-of-developing-collaborative-teams-for-future-success

Chapter 4

Terry Borton, *Reach, touch, and teach: Student concerns and process education.*

Carmody, B. (2015). 3 reasons celebrating your many accomplishments is critical to your success. *Inc.* Retrieved from https://www.inc.com/bill-carmody/3-reasons-celebrating-your-many-accomplishments-is-critical-to-your-success.html

Pete Hall & Alisa Simeral, *Creating a Culture of Reflective Practice: Building Capacity for Schoolwide Success.*

Chapter 5

Bain & Company. (2018). Mission and vision statements. Retrieved from https://www.bain.com/insights/management-tools-mission-and-vision-statements/

Stephen Covey, *7 Habits of Highly Effective People.*

Haughey, D. (2014). A brief history of SMART goals. Retrieved from https://www.projectsmart.co.uk/brief-history-of-smart-goals.php

Brandon, J. (2016). 6 ways great leadership Is exactly like gardening. Retrieved from https://www.inc.com/john-brandon/6-ways-great-leadership-is-exactly-like-gardening.html

ACKNOWLEDGMENTS

We express a deep sense of gratitude to our families, friends, mentors and colleagues who have helped us learn and grow as everyday leaders.

Special thanks to our spouses, Tecara and Brandon. Thank you both for the sacrifices you each made and the unwavering support as we worked together for hours on end to create this work. We love you.

Many thanks to Tecara, Teia, and Shanique. Your feedback, edits, suggestions, and encouragement during this process is greatly appreciated. The book would not be what it is without you.

ABOUT THE AUTHORS

Full Bios:

Dr. Willie Jones is a leadership development professional with over a decade of experience designing and delivering high impact and engaging learning solutions. In professional roles, he has served as High School Teacher, Community College Instructor, Instructional Designer for University Professors, Training Consultant to a Fortune 250 organization, and Regional Training Director responsible for the North American region. His B.S. Degree was earned at North Carolina State University. Years later, he furthered his education at North Carolina Agricultural & Technical State University where he earned a M.S. Degree in Adult Education and PhD Degree in Leadership.

Dr. Tempestt Adams is an educator, workshop facilitator, and professional speaker. She holds a Ph.D. in Curriculum & Instruction from the University of North Carolina at Charlotte, a general MBA from Pfeiffer University, and a bachelor's in Business & Marketing Education from North Carolina State University. Her specialty area is Career and Technical Education (CTE) and she has over ten years of teaching and leadership experience across the middle school, high school, community college, and university levels. While CTE encompasses a plethora of topics and subjects, at its core its focus is on career development skills.

To book the team for training, workshops, or speaking engagements, visit www.jonesadamsconsulting.com.